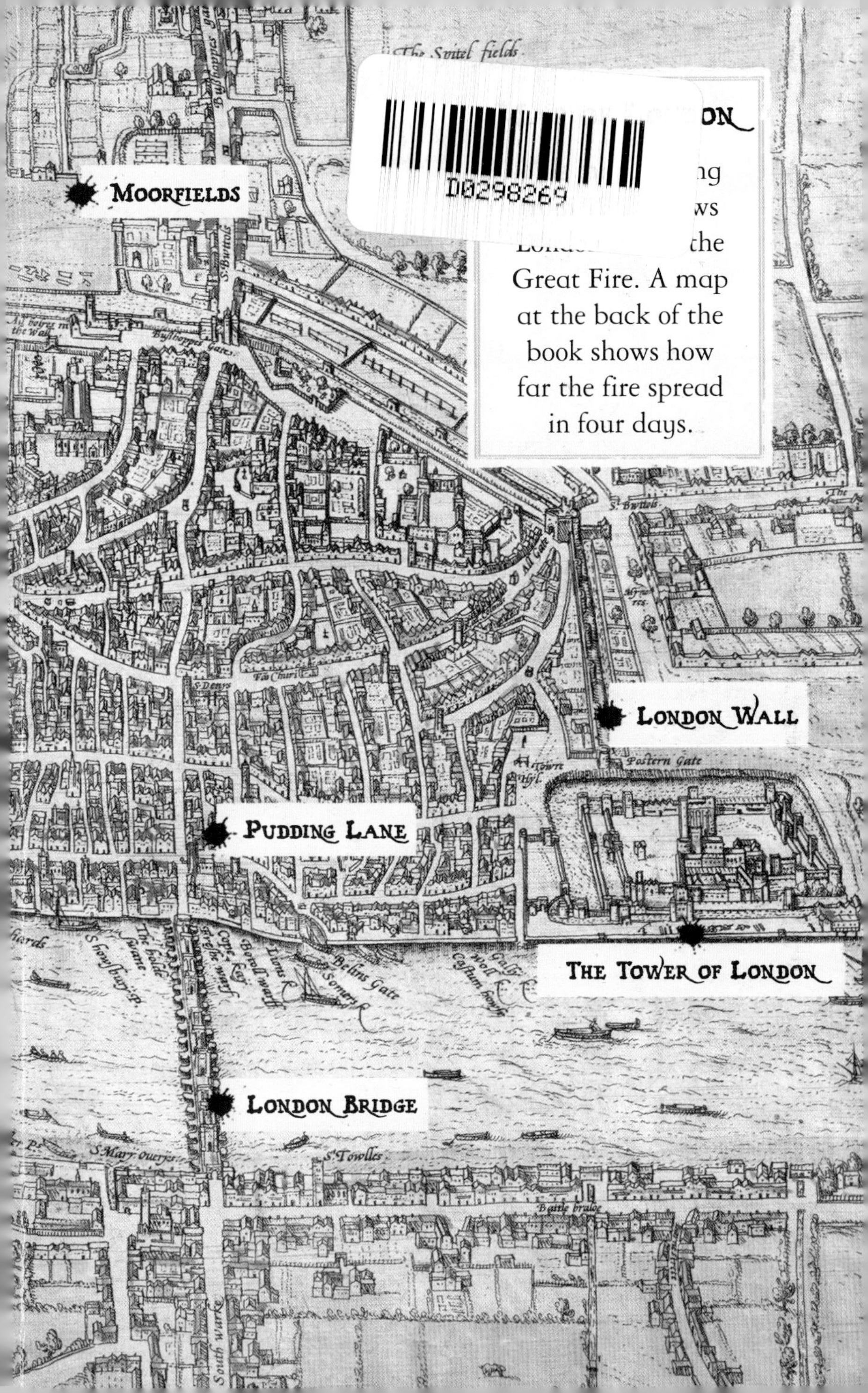
Great Fire. A map
at the back of the
book shows how
far the fire spread
in four days.
Moorfields
London Wall
Pudding Lane
The Tower of London
London Bridge
The Spitel fields
Postern Gate
S. Towlles

The Great Fire of London

Susanna Davidson
Illustrated by Rick Fairlamb

Reading consultant: Alison Kelly

Contents

Chapter 1

The old city

On Saturday September 1, 1666, dawn broke bright and clear over the city of London.

No one who gazed at the view that morning knew it was the last sunrise the old city would ever see.

The streets, enclosed by the old Roman city wall, were winding and narrow.

Wooden houses jutted outwards, their roofs nearly touching. Horses and carts jammed the alleyways.

Waste blocked open drains, its stench mingling with the reek of rotting vegetable peel.

There was fear in the air, too – fear of invasion. England was at war with the Dutch. That morning, one hundred English ships were sailing towards the coast of Holland, ready to attack the Dutch fleet.

Worse still was the fear of the plague. The year before, one in five Londoners had died from the disease. Over the long, hot summer, the death toll had begun to rise again.

But that bright, clear September morning, busy Londoners were going about their business as usual.

Around the Tower of London, ironmongers were laying out their wares.

Traders thronged to the meat market at Leadenhall, while fishmongers and poultry-sellers flocked to Greenyard next door.

And on Pudding Lane, just to the north of the river, cooks and bakers were busy selling their food.

By eight or nine that evening, one baker on Pudding Lane, Thomas Farriner, was closing up his shop.

The oven was nearly cold. He checked it and placed a bundle of sticks close by, ready to light the fire the next morning. Then he went to bed.

As he slept, a stray spark from the embers in the oven lit the sticks. They began to burn. Around two o'clock that morning, his servant woke, choking on the smoke that filled the ground floor.

Hardly able to breathe, he stumbled upstairs to wake his master. The Great Fire of London had begun.

Chapter 2

Pudding Lane

Smoke and flames filled the house. There was no way down. Thomas, his daughter Hanna, his manservant and the maid huddled together at the top of the stairs.

"We'll have to climb out of the window," said Thomas, "and crawl along the guttering. Then we can climb back in through the window next door."

One by one, they made their way to safety, but their maid was too scared, or confused by the smoke, to follow them. The fire had claimed its first victim.

There was no fire service to call. As the fire spread, the churchbells were rung as a warning to other Londoners.

People tried to put out the fire using buckets of water collected from the river. But they were no match for the flames.

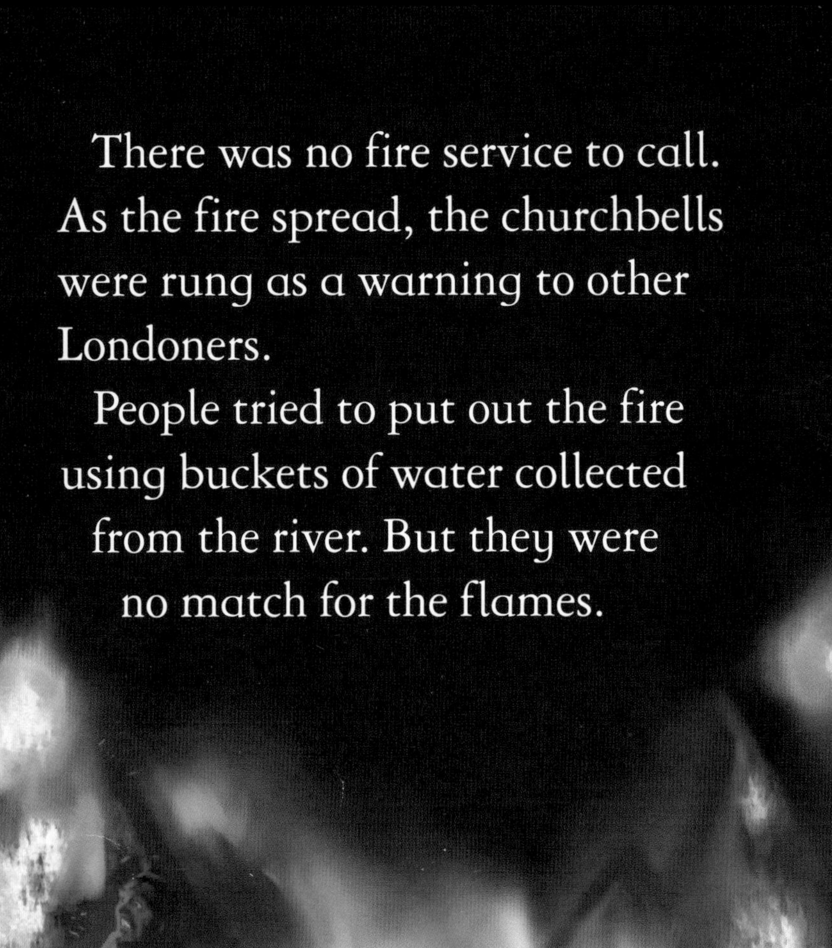

The local constables soon arrived and realized more needed to be done. The only answer, they said, was to pull down the surrounding houses, to stop the fire from spreading.

Within an hour, Thomas Bludworth, the Mayor of London, was called. The fire, fanned by the strong easterly wind, was spreading fast.

Flames were eagerly engulfing the nearby houses, but Bludworth didn't think it was that serious... and went back home to sleep.

Seven streets away, Samuel Pepys, who worked for the government, and his wife, Elisabeth, were woken by their maid with news of the fire.

"Nothing to worry about," said Pepys, watching the glow from his window. Then, like Bludworth, he went back to bed.

Urged on by the wind, the fire tore from street to street. By dawn, it had consumed 300 houses, and reached London Bridge.

When Pepys woke the next morning, he was amazed to see the fire still burning. He rushed to the Tower of London and climbed the battlements to get a better look.

Far off, he could see the fire raging... and steadily coming closer.

Appalled by what he saw, he hired a boat to take him upriver. From there, he realized the true extent of the fire – and that it threatened the whole city.

A large part of the north bank of the river was burning. People were flinging their belongings into boats, or just into the river itself.

Pigeons, which Londoners kept for food, fluttered above their burning homes, until the leaping flames singed their wings.

Even as Pepys watched, one of the city's tallest churches caught light. Within minutes, its burning steeple toppled over and crashed into the street below.

Pepys decided he had to get to the palace at Whitehall at once, to see the King.

Chapter 3

Fear and flames

Bewildered and scared, most people weren't trying to fight the fire. Instead they were fleeing through the city gates with all the belongings they could take.

They used wagons, handcarts or carried their things on their backs. The sick were hauled through the streets, still in their beds.

When King Charles II heard the news of the fire from Pepys, he ordered people to start pulling down houses.

"Lord, what can I do?" cried the Mayor, in the midst of it all. "We have started pulling down houses. But the fire overtakes us faster than we can work."

In despair, the Mayor went home, while the wind carried the sparks from the flames far and wide, spreading the fire further still.

The King demanded that more and more buildings be pulled down, in a desperate attempt to stop the fire. He also called in troops for support.

But the wind was working as his enemy. It began blowing north, then south, pushing the flames into the middle of the city.

By Sunday afternoon, the fire had reached the warehouses along the Thames. Full of oil, sugar, butter and brandy, they fed the flames, turning the fire into a raging inferno.

As dusk came, the sky was still bright and yellow. Pepys wrote in his diary of, “a most horrid malicious bloody flame.” That night, he watched his city burn, and wept.

By Monday, the fire was as strong as ever, eating up building after building, leaving devastation in its path.

It tore down alleys and leaped from street to street. The Thames was covered in boats and barges as more and more people tried to flee.

In the open fields to the north of the city, people were setting up makeshift tents and little shelters.

That night there was no darkness. One man, John Evelyn, wrote of, "The noise and crackling and thunder... the shrieking of women and children..."

On the streets, fear had made people turn to violence. England's enemies, the Dutch and the French, were blamed for starting the fire. Foreigners venturing out were attacked by mobs.

Belongings were stolen and some people went crazy with fear. One man even set fire to his own house.

Pepys was determined to save his possessions. He borrowed a cart, packed up his valuables and rode through the night in his dressing gown to his friend's house, further away to the east.

Smoke from the fire now stretched for fifty miles outside London. People leaving the city could travel for hours in its shadow.

The following day, Tuesday, the fire raged worse than ever. Pepys spent the evening digging a pit in his garden, to bury his wine and his prized parmesan cheese.

By now, the fire was heading towards London's most famous landmark: St. Paul's Cathedral.

To many, it seemed unthinkable that the cathedral could burn. Its walls were thick and made of stone. But the cathedral was covered in wooden scaffolding for repairs...

The fire crept closer and closer across the churchyard, until sparks caught the scaffolding.

On his way home, schoolboy William Taswell watched from a mile away. At eight o'clock, he saw flames appear on the lead roof.

The fire spread fast, melting the lead, so that it dripped down into the cathedral.

The stonework cracked, and then exploded under the heat.

The lead ran down the hill in a stream, glowing fiery red. Next, the books, packed tightly into the crypt for safety, caught alight.

At that moment, the whole building went up in a huge blaze that lit the entire sky.

It was bright enough for William to pull a book from his pocket and read the words on the page.

That night, the moon turned blood red. But, at long last, the wind was dying down.

Chapter 4

Fighting the fire

The long, hot summer had left London's wooden houses bone dry, and ripe for burning.

All people had to fight the fire were leather buckets and wooden ladders...

...along with small fire squirts (little more than giant syringes), and iron fire hooks to pull down the houses.

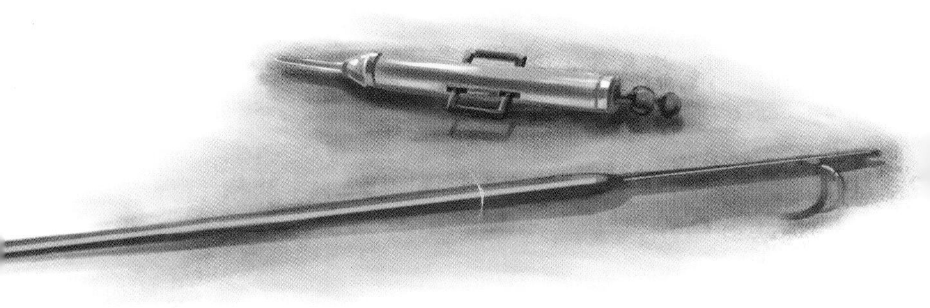

The fire engines were simply wooden carts filled with water. But the men pushing the carts couldn't reach the fires in time. The narrow streets were too busy with people fleeing the flames.

The waterwheels at London Bridge had also been burned, so there was no water supply for much of the city.

Early on Monday morning, the King's brother, the Duke of York, had taken command of fighting the fire.

He set up 'fire posts' – groups of soldiers and volunteers. The King then rode around the city, encouraging them as they pulled down houses.

For two and a half days, the Duke's men fought the flames. They lit trails of gunpowder, blowing up the houses that lay in the fire's path.

Even as the wind quietened on Wednesday, the King was sure he'd lose his palace at Whitehall, and fears grew for Westminster Abbey.

The Duke responded by getting everyone he could find to fight the fire.

By Wednesday afternoon, it seemed as if they were winning. There were still fires burning all over London, but without the wind to feed the flames, they were being held in check.

By now, 13,200 houses had been destroyed. Eighty-seven churches had burned down, and around 80,000 people had lost their homes.

Many of the homeless, rich and poor, were camped in the fields around London, far to the east and the north.

Much of the city's food supply had burned with the houses, so there wasn't a lot to eat.

Then, on Wednesday night in one of the camps, word spread that the fire had been started by the Dutch.

It was claimed that thousands of French and Dutch soldiers were marching on London. Within minutes, there was panic.

People grabbed knives and whatever weapons they could find, and headed out to save their city.

The angry mob didn't make it far, before they were pushed back to the fields by the Duke's soldiers.

The next morning, the King himself rode out to Moorfields, to proclaim the fire an accident, not a plot.

Back in the city, the clear-up operation had begun.

Everywhere were ashes and glowing timbers. The ground was almost too hot to walk on.

William Taswell, setting out to look at the ruins of St. Paul's, began to feel dizzy in the warm air. 'A black darkness' covered the sky, he wrote later.

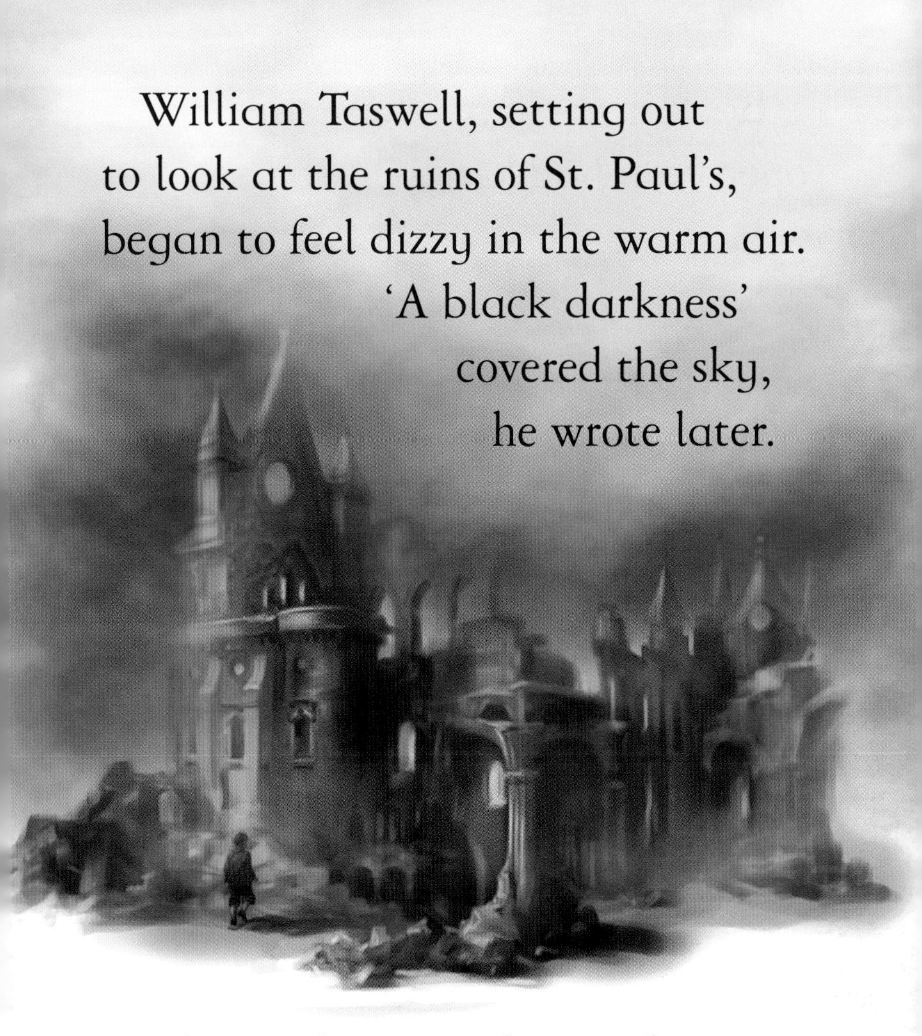

John Evelyn, wandering the streets on Friday, was almost overcome by smoke and fumes and "even burnt the soles of my shoes."

"There is nothing to be seen but heaps of stones," wrote one eyewitness.

The skyline had changed forever. From the south bank of the Thames, you could see right into the heart of London.

Amazingly, only ten people are recorded as having died in the fire. One, an elderly watchmaker, refused to leave his home and died when his house collapsed on top of him.

One thing was certain. London would never be the same again.

Chapter 5

Rebuilding the city

On September 13, one week after the fire ended, the King declared he wanted to see "a much more beautiful city" rise from the ashes of old London.

New rules were passed to make the city more resistant to fire. There were to be no more wooden houses. Everything was to be made of brick or stone, and some streets widened, so that fire couldn't spread from one side to the other.

Swiftly, ambitious town planners presented the King with their ideas.

The King was most keen on an architect named Christopher Wren. Wren's vision for a new London was on a grand scale.

But none of the schemes were carried out. They were too costly and would have taken too long.

The homeless urgently needed rehousing, and there were also churches, inns, shops and warehouses to rebuild.

In the end, most buildings were rebuilt on their original sites.

It took about fifty years to rebuild the city. St. Paul's Cathedral, redesigned by Christopher Wren, wasn't completed until 1711.

Wren also designed a monument to the fire. It stands 61m (202ft) high – the same distance from the Monument to the bakery in Pudding Lane, where the fire first began.

At the top is a flaming golden urn, and a view over the city reborn.

Timeline of the Great Fire

Sunday 2nd September, 1666

1am

Fire breaks out in Thomas Farriner's bakery.

6am

The fire reaches London Bridge, having destroyed around 300 houses.

Camps are set up around the city for the homeless.

Tuesday 4th September

Morning

King Charles rides through the city, urging people to fight the flames.

Evening

The fire is 300 yards away from the Tower of London. Houses are blown up with gunpowder, to stop the fire from reaching the Tower.

A story spreads that the fire was started by Dutch and French soldiers.

Thursday 6th September

5am

The last outbreak of fire is put out at Bishopsgate.

Afternoon

The Great Fire of London is over.

8am

Samuel Pepys views the fire from a boat on the Thames.

10am

Pepys travels to Whitehall to warn King Charles II about the fire.

MONDAY 3RD SEPTEMBER

9am

The Duke of York takes command of fighting the fire. Teams pull down houses, to stop the flames from spreading.

8pm

St. Paul's Cathedral catches fire.

WEDNESDAY 5TH SEPTEMBER

Evening

The wind starts to settle, so the flames stop spreading.

1675

Work begins on the new St. Paul's Cathedral, and continues until 1711.

1677

Wren's 'Monument' is completed, remembering the Great Fire of London.

Usborne Quicklinks

For links to websites to find out more about the Great Fire of London, go to the Usborne Quicklinks website at **www.usborne.com/quicklinks** and type in the keywords 'great fire'.

Please follow the internet safety guidelines at the Usborne Quicklinks website. Usborne Publishing cannot be responsible for any website other than its own.

History expert: Meriel Jeater, Museum of London
Edited by Rob Lloyd Jones
Designed by Samantha Barrett
Digital manipulation by Nick Wakeford
Series editor: Lesley Sims
Series designer: Russell Punter

First published in 2015 by Usborne Publishing Ltd., Usborne House, 83-85 Saffron Hill, London EC1N 8RT, England. www.usborne.com

Clarkenwell
S Giles
Smythe Fyeld
St. Paul's Cathedral
Whyt freres
Bridwell
Blak freres
Benams Castle
Powles warf
Brakenwarf
Quene hyve
Thre Crane
Parys Gardeyn
The Bowll bay tyng
The Beare bayting